The Big Cookbook

of Delicious and

Exotic Bengali

Meals

A Compilation of Bengali Recipes

Table of Contents

Introduction

The Bengali cuisine is an amazing cuisine that suits a lot of diets. If you are a vegetarian, the Bengali cuisine has a lot of vegetables-themed recipes that you can try out.

Also, if you're a non-vegetarian, there are more than enough recipes that you can indulge in under the Bengali cuisine.

Boasting of an abundance of fish, spices and rice as a staple, the Bengali cuisine is flavorful to a fault.

The Bengals love their cuisine a little too much, and you are about to find out why. With the aid of this recipe book, you will be introduced to delicious Bengali recipes.

So, come with me as we unveil and explore different Bengali recipes for your delight, starting with the Breakfast Mughlai Paratha.

This egg meal is like no other!!!

Bengali people have full days, and they begin them with the most exotic of breakfast recipes...

1 – Radha Ballabhi

Makes: 6 Servings

Cooking + Prep Time: 55 minutes

The list of ingredients:

- 1 tsp. of asafetida
- 1 tsp. of ginger paste
- 1 tsp. of roasted, crushed fennel seeds
- vegetable Oil
- 1 tsp. of black cumin seeds

- 1 cup of flour, all-purpose
- Sugar, as desired
- 1 tsp. of red chili powder
- Salt, as desired
- 1 cup of Ardar dal

Method:

Step 1

Grind the turmeric powder along with fennel powder and ground asafetida.

Step 2

Heat 2 tbsp. oil in medium pan. Add ginger paste, black cumin and 1 pinch salt. Fry for 5-10 seconds.

Step 3

Add tur dal paste, red chili powder, 1 tsp. salt and 1 tsp. sugar. Cook over flame.

Step 4

When water in mixture has dried, remove from flame. Stir continuously so mixture won't stick to pan.

Step 5

To prepare the dough, pour flour in bowl. Add 2 tsp. sugar and 1 tsp. salt.

Step 6

Add 1 cup warm water. Knead well. Kneading needs to be done 20-25 minutes before you make dough poori.

Step 7

Create round dough of flour. Fill prepared stuffing material into it. Press lightly between your palms. Close them and roll.

Step 8

Heat the oil in pan. Puri edges should be well cooked on both sides.

Step 9

Serve with masala potato, curd or tamarind sauce.

2 – Luchi and Cholar Dal

Makes: 4 Servings

Cooking + Prep Time: 35 minutes

The list of ingredients:

- 3 to 4 cloves
- 1 tsp. of chopped green chilies
- 1 tsp. of cumin seeds
- 1 inch of cinnamon

- Salt, as desired

- 2 tbsp. of raisins

- 1 tsp. of grated ginger

- 1 tsp. of granulated sugar

- 1/4 cup of thinly sliced fresh coconut

- 2 to 3 green cardamom pods

- 1/2 tsp. of turmeric powder

- 4 to 5 red, dry chilies

- 1/2 tsp. of Hing

- 1 cup of Chana Dal

- 3 tbsp. of ghee

- 2 bay leaves

Method:

Step 1

Wash dal. Add it to pressure cooker with three cups water, plus salt and turmeric powder.

Step 2

Cook in pressure cooker till barely done. Don't allow dal to become mushy.

Step 3

Heat the ghee for tempering.

Step 4

Add the coconut slices. Fry till golden brown. Place slices on plate.

Step 5

Add hing and cumin seeds to same ghee. Allow to crackle for several seconds.

Step 6

Add dry chilies, cinnamon, gloves, bay leaf and green cardamom and fry for several seconds.

Step 7

Add green chili and ginger. Fry for a few more seconds.

Step 8

Pour tempering over deal with sugar, raisins and fried coconut. Combine well. Serve hot.

3 – Breakfast Mughlai Paratha

Makes: 8 Servings

Cooking + Prep Time: 40 minutes

The list of ingredients:

For dough:

- 1 cup of whole milk
- sea salt, as desired

- 1 1/10 lbs. of whole wheat flour

For filling

- 3 eggs, large
- 1 1/10 lbs. of spicy minced meat (called Masala Kheema)

To fry: sunflower or vegetable oil

Method:

Step 1

Mix flour and dash of salt in large sized bowl. Add milk slowly. Knead well. Once you have used up the milk, add water and knead to create smooth, medium-soft dough.

Step 2

Wet hands. Rub along dough surface. Cover with damp cloth. Set aside for 12-15 minutes.

Step 3

Whisk salt and eggs and set them aside.

Step 4

Divide dough in balls. Press flat. Roll balls out on floured cutting board in four-inch circles.

Step 5

Place large spoonful of spicy minced meat in middle of circles. Fold edges of circles in to cover meat filling and seal it. Pinch folds and shut well.

Step 6

Press gently on filled balls to flatten them, then roll them gently into six-inch circles. Set them aside.

Step 7

Place circles one over the next with sheets of cling wrap between them so they won't stick.

Step 8

Heat griddle over med. flame. Place paratha on griddle. Cook till you can see small bubbles on top, then flip it. Wait to see bubbles in that side. Brush with oil. Flip it again. Brush with egg. Flip again. Grease other side. Brush egg on it, too. When both sides have cooked, start next paratha. Repeat with all dough and filling and serve.

Visit the dusty back streets of
Bengali for authentic Bengali
lunch, dinner, side dish and
appetizer recipes...

4 – Bengali Chicken Curry

Makes: 4 Servings

Cooking + Prep Time: 1 hour 35 minutes

The list of ingredients:

- 1 tsp. of ground cumin
- 1 tsp. of curry powder
- 2 large, chopped red-skinned potatoes

- 1 tbsp. of garlic-ginger paste
- 4 bite-size cubed, halved chicken breasts, boneless, skinless
- 1 tsp. of garam masala spice blend
- 1 tsp. of ground turmeric
- 2 large, diced tomatoes
- 2 large, diced onions
- 1 tsp. of cayenne, +/- as desired
- 2 tbsp. of olive oil
- 1/2 cup of fresh cilantro

Method:

Step 1

Heat oil in large sized skillet on med high. Stir and cook onions in oil till they are translucent, usually five minutes or so.

Step 2

Add garlic-ginger paste. Continue to cook for five more minutes. Lower heat down to med. Stir tomatoes into mixture. Cook till tomatoes become pulpy, or five to 10 minutes.

Step 3

Use cumin, turmeric, garam masala, curry powder

and cayenne pepper to season. Cook for five more
minutes.

Step 4

Add potatoes and chicken to skillet mixture. Stir
occasionally while simmering till potatoes become
tender and chicken isn't pink in middle anymore,
usually 20 minutes or so.

Step 5

Sprinkle mixture with cilantro. Continue to simmer
for 10 more minutes and serve hot.

5 – Bengali Spicy Shrimp

Makes: 4 Servings

Cooking + Prep Time: 40 minutes

The list of ingredients:

- 1/4 cup of fresh cilantro leaves
- 1 tsp. of mild garlic paste
- 2 chopped onions
- Sea salt, as desired

- 1/2 tsp. of garam masala spice blend
- 1 chopped tomato
- 1/2 tsp. of ground turmeric
- 2 tbsp. of vegetable oil
- 1 lb. of peeled, de-veined shrimp
- 2 de-seeded, minced chili peppers, green

Method:

Step 1

Heat the oil on med-high in large sized skillet. Stir while cooking onions till they are golden brown in color, usually eight minutes or so. Add and stir tomatoes, then cook for two to three minutes.

Step 2

Add and stir chili peppers, garam masala, turmeric, garlic paste a bit of sea salt into mixture. Cook for two more minutes.

Step 3

Reduce the heat down to low. Add shrimp. Stir while cooking on low heat till shrimp appear bright pink outside and meat in center isn't transparent anymore, usually eight minutes or so. Add just a bit of water as needed. You want a thick sauce. Use cilantro to sprinkle and serve.

6 – Mustard Curry

Makes :4 Servings

Cooking + Prep Time: 35 minutes

The list of ingredients:

- 5 green chilies
- 1/2 tsp. of red chili powder
- Sea salt, as needed
- 1 1/2 diced onion

- 4 pieces of rohu fish
- 3 tbsp. of mustard paste
- 1 tsp. of turmeric powder
- 1 pinch of black onion seeds
- 3 tbsp. of mustard oil

Method:

Step 1

Soak the mustard powder in 1/2 cup filtered water with a bit of salt for 12-15 minutes. Mix well in grinder.

Step 2

Heat oil in pan. Marinate fish in turmeric and salt. Deep fry it. Remove to dish.

Step 3

Add onion seeds to remaining oil. Allow them to crackle. Add onions. Fry till lightly browned.

Step 4

Add mustard paste. Don't allow skin of mustard to be included.

Step 5

Add salt, chili powder and turmeric powder. Cook for a couple minutes.

Step 6

Add 1/2 cup of filtered water. Add fish gradually. Bring to boil till you have a thicker consistency. Use green chilies and 1 tbsp. mustard oil to garnish. Serve while hot.

7 – Bengali Potato Egg Curry

Makes: 2 Servings

Cooking + Prep Time: 1 hour

The list of ingredients:

- 2 tsp. of ground coriander

- 3 tbsp. of vegetable oil

- 1 tsp. of ground cumin

- 2 cups of filtered water

- 2 small green chili peppers

- 6 quartered hard-boiled eggs

- 3 quartered tomatoes

- 1 cooked, then peeled and 1"-cubed potato, large

- 1/2 tsp. of cayenne pepper, +/- as desired

- 2 tsp. of garlic paste

- 2 peeled, quartered medium onions

- 1 tsp. garam masala spice blend

- Sea salt, as desired

- 2 tsp. of ginger paste

- 1/2 tsp. of ground turmeric

Optional: 2 tbsp. of fresh chopped cilantro

Method:

Step 1

Heat 1 tbsp. of oil in skillet on med. heat. Add and stir onions and cook till they are translucent and soft. Reduce the heat down to med-low and continue to cook, while occasionally stirring, till onions turn golden in color.

Step 2

Remove skillet from the heat. Set aside. Transfer the onions to bowl of food processor. Blend chilies, onions and tomatoes into smooth-textured paste.

Step 3

Next, heat remaining 2 tbsp. of oil in skillet on med. heat. Add the onion mixture and be careful, since it can splatter. Stir while cooking for two to three minutes more.

Step 4

Add and stir ginger and garlic pastes, cumin, coriander, turmeric, garam masala, salt and cayenne pepper. Stir while cooking till oil starts separating from mixture, usually at five minutes or so.

Step 5

Pour filtered water into the skillet. Bring the sauce to boil. Add potato cubes. Stir in eggs gently.

Step 6

Reduce the heat down to low. Simmer till sauce thickens a bit, usually 10 minutes or so. Remove pan from heat. Use cilantro to garnish. Serve.

8 – Potato Curry

Makes: 2-3 Servings

Cooking + Prep Time: 35 minutes

The list of ingredients:

- granulated sugar
- 1 tbsp. of paanch-phoron (found at Indian stores)
- 4 or 5 cubed potatoes, medium
- 1 pinch Hing

- Sea salt

- 2 or 3 whole, dry red chilies

Method:

Step 1

Heat the oil in pan. Temper with red chilies, paanch phoron and Hing. Allow to sizzle, then add potato cubes. Fry potatoes over med. heat but don't allow them to brown.

Step 2

Add sugar and salt as desired. Add water to cover them. Cover pan. Cook until potatoes have become soft but still are holding their shapes. All water needs to evaporate before removing pan from heat. Serve.

9 – Bengali Fish Curry

Makes: 4 Servings

Cooking + Prep Time: 1 1/2 hour

The list of ingredients:

For marinade

- 1 tbsp. of canola oil
- 4 chopped garlic cloves

- 1/2 cup of chopped tomatoes

- 1/2 tsp. of sea salt

- 1 chopped onion

- 1 tsp. of ground coriander

- 1 x 1" piece of fresh peeled, chopped ginger root

- 2 tsp. of Dijon mustard

- 2 tbsp. of canola oil

- 1 tsp. of white sugar

- 1/4 cup of vegetable broth

- 1 tsp. of sea salt

- 5 halved cashews

- 1/2 tsp. of ground turmeric

- 1/4 cup of fresh chopped cilantro

- 1 tsp. of ground pepper

- 4 white fish fillets

- 1 tsp. of ground cumin

- 2 tsp. of cayenne pepper, as desired

Method:

Step 1

Mix 2 tbsp. oil, 1/2 tsp. sea salt, pepper, and mustard in shallow bowl. Add fish fillets and coat well. Marinate fish in fridge for 1/2 hour.

Step 2

Combine cashews, ginger, garlic and onion in food processor. Pulse till paste is formed.

Step 3

Preheat oven to 350F.

Step 4

Heat 1 tbsp. oil in skillet on med low. Add prepared paste. Stir while cooking for one to two minutes. Add sugar, 1 tsp. salt, coriander cumin, turmeric and cayenne pepper. Stir while cooking for five more minutes. Add in broth and tomatoes.

Step 5

Arrange fish in baking dish. Top with sauce. Cover dish. Bake in 350F oven till fish will easily flake with fork. Use chopped cilantro to garnish. Serve.

10 – Bengali Dhal

Makes: 4 Servings

Cooking + Prep Time: 50 minutes

The list of ingredients:

- 1 tbsp. of vegetable oil
- 1 cup of red lentils
- 1 medium bay leaf
- 1/2 tsp. of sea salt

- 3 cups of filtered water
- 4 chopped garlic cloves
- 2 x 2" whole serrano peppers
- 1 cup of sliced onions
- 1/2 tsp. of ground turmeric
- 2 tbsp. of chopped cilantro
- 3/4 cup of cherry tomatoes

Method:

Step 1

Wash lentils in strainer. Combine them with water in pan on med high. Add garlic and 1/2 onion slices. Reserve rest of onions. Stir in salt, tomatoes, bay leaf and turmeric.

Step 2

Add chilies. When mixture starts boiling, reduce heat to simmer. Cook till lentils have broken apart and thickened a bit, usually 20 minutes or so.

Step 3

Heat oil on med. heat in skillet till oil starts shimmering. Add reserved onion slices. Str and cook till onions have softened and become translucent, five minutes or so.

Step 4

Reduce heat down to med low. Continue to stir and cook till onion is dark brown and quite tender, about 15 minutes more. Stir in remainder of garlic. Stir constantly while cooking till garlic is tender and fragrant, usually two minutes or so.

Step 5

Pour skillet contents into lentils. Stir well. Use cilantro to garnish. Serve.

11 – Bengali Lamb Gravy

Makes: 6 Servings

Cooking + Prep Time: 1 hour 10 minutes

The list of ingredients:

- Sea salt, as desired

- 2 lbs. of 1" boneless cubed lamb shoulder

- 1 chopped medium onion

- 1/2 tsp. of garam masala spice mixture

- 2 tbsp. of unsalted butter

Optional: 1/2 tsp. of ground turmeric

- 1/2 cup of heavy cream
- 1/2 tsp. of cayenne pepper, +/- as desired
- 1 cup of fresh chopped cilantro
- 1 tbsp. of tomato paste
- 1/2 tsp. of minced garlic
- 1 cup of filtered water
- 1/2 tsp. of minced ginger
- 1 tbsp. of pure honey

Method:

Step 1

Season lamb with sea salt and garam masala. Heat 1 tbsp. butter in large sized skillet on med. heat. Fry cubed lamb till browned, while constantly stirring. Remove from skillet. Set it aside.

Step 2

Melt the rest of the butter in same skillet on med. heat. Add onion. Stir and cook till onion turns translucent and softens, usually five minutes or so.

Step 3

Add and stir garlic, turmeric and ginger into pan. Stir while cooking for one minute. Add and stir tomato paste and cayenne in till blended well. Add water and stir. Bring water to simmer. Return lamb cubes to skillet. Simmer on low heat for 15-20 minutes, till the lamb has become tender.

Step 4

Add and stir honey and cream into mixture. Transfer to serving dish. Use cilantro to garnish and serve.

12 – Aloo Posto

Makes 3 Servings

Cooking + Prep Time: 35 minutes

The list of ingredients:

- 1/2 tsp. of onion seeds
- 4 medium green chilies
- 1/2 tsp. of ground turmeric
- 5 tbsp. of poppy seeds
- 2 tbsp. of mustard oil

- 1 tsp. of sea salt

- 1 tbsp. of filtered water

- 4 large potatoes

Method:

Step 1

Soak poppy seeds in filtered water for 25 to 30 minutes. Make them into a paste with a thick consistency.

Step 2

Add 2 to 3 chilies and a bit of salt. Paste should remain thick.

Step 3

Chop potatoes into small sized cubes. Wash them well.

Step 4

Heat oil in wok. Add the onion seeds.

Step 5

Add potatoes to oil. Fry over med. flame for three to four minutes. Add green chilies, turmeric and a bit of sea salt. Combine well.

Step 6

Add a cup of filtered water to pan and cover it. When mixture is half-finished cooking, add poppy seed

paste. Cook until the potatoes have completely
softened. Mix again.

Step 7

Cook until water has been completely evaporated.
Serve hot over rice.

13 – Hilsa Curry

Makes: 4 Servings

Cooking + Prep Time: 1 hour 5 minutes

The list of ingredients:

- 1/2 cup of mustard oil
- 17 1/2 oz. of sliced washed, dried iilish fish
- 4 green chilies
- 1 tsp. of black cumin seeds

- 2 cups of boiled water

- 2 pinches of sea salt

- 1 tsp. of powdered turmeric

Method:

Step 1

Wash fish. Slice in pieces.

Step 2

Marinate fish with turmeric and salt. Set aside.

Step 3

Heat some of the oil in pan. Fry marinated fish in shallow oil till pieces are golden in color.

Step 4

Heat rest of oil in separate pan. Add cumin seeds. Slit chilies. Add to oil and continue to stir.

Step 5

Add fish to oil. Add boiled water. Add turmeric and salt as desired. Bring to boil. Allow to cook for several minutes. Serve while hot over rice.

14 – Mochar Chop

Makes: 1-2 Servings

Cooking + Prep Time: 5 minutes

The list of ingredients:

For mocha

- 1 large, chopped onion
- Sugar, granulated, as desired
- 1 cup of filtered water

- 10 to 12 peeled, roasted, halved peanuts

- 2 tbsp. of corn flour

- 2 medium boiled, peeled potatoes

- 3 tbsp. of shredded coconut

- 1 tsp. of powdered garam masala spice mix

- 1 tbsp. of garlic-ginger paste

- 2 chopped green chilies

- Sea salt, as desired

To coat: breadcrumbs

To fry: Oil, as needed

Method:

Step 1

Mash potatoes and add mocha.

Step 2

Add garam masala, green chilies, peanuts, coconut, garlic-ginger paste, chopped onions, sugar and salt. Use your hands to mash ingredients together.

Step 3

Heat 1 tbsp. oil in pan. Transfer mixture to pan. Fry for five to six minutes, till mixture is dry. Remove from the pan. Allow to cool.

Step 4

Mix corn flour and water in small bowl to create batter.

Step 5

Take small balls of mixture in hand. Shape like cutlets or chops. Dip in corn flour batter. Roll them in breadcrumbs.

Step 6

Heat the oil in heavy pan over med high. Once oil is heated, lower heat to med. Fry chops till they are golden brown in color. Remove to paper towels.

Step 7

Serve with Bengali mustard sauce or ketchup.

15 – Dhokar Dalna

Makes: 8 Servings

Cooking + Prep Time: 55 minutes

The list of ingredients:

- 1 cup of yellow moong dal

- 1 tsp. of caraway seeds

- 1/2 tsp. of ground nutmeg

- 2 green cardamom pods

- 1 tsp. of powdered garam masala spice blend

- 4 cloves

- 4 green chilies

- 1 stick of cinnamon

- 4 green cardamom pods

- Sugar, granulated, as needed

- 1 tsp. of powdered coriander

- 2 bay leaves

- 3 tsp. of red chili powder

- 1 cup of filtered water

- 1 tsp. of ground turmeric

- 1 handful of fresh coriander leaves

- 3 tsp. of mild ginger paste

- 1/2 tsp. of thymol seeds

- Sea salt, as desired

- 1 tsp. of black peppercorns

- 1/2 cup of light yogurt

- 1 tsp. of powdered cumin

- 1/2 tsp. of asafetida

- 1/2 tbsp. of clarified unsalted butter

- 2 tsp. of cumin seeds

- 2 cloves

- 1/2 quart of mustard oil

- 1 tbsp. of green chilies, crushed into paste
- 1/2 cup of pureed tomatoes

Method:

Step 1

Use-soaked lentils, salt, and green chilies to make paste.

Step 2

Heat 3/4 tbsp. oil in pan. Add 1 1/2 tsp. ginger paste, asafetida, thymol seeds and cumin seeds. Sauté at med-high flame till moisture has disappeared and the oil has separated.

Step 3

Add lentil paste. Adjust sugar and salt as desired. Continue to combine and fold mixture till it leaves sides of pan and takes on a consistency like dough.

Step 4

Grease large, flat dish. Spread contents from pan on it.

Step 5

Smooth surface of mixture. Once completely cooled, cut diamond shaped lentil cakes out.

Step 6

Heat the oil on med. flame in wok. When oil has heated, begin to deep fry cakes in small batches.

Step 7

Heat 2/3 tbsp. oil. Add cloves, cardamom, cinnamon, cumin seeds and bay leaves. Make paste using chili powder, turmeric, coriander leaves and cumin. Add paste to oil and sauté thoroughly.

Step 8

Add rest of ginger paste to pan. Sauté till all moisture has disappeared. Add pureed tomatoes. Fold and mix all ingredients. Cook till done. Adjust seasonings as desired. Add 1 cup filtered water. Bring to boil.

Step 9

Add 1 tsp. garam masala, yogurt and chilies. Stir and add lentil patties. Add some chopped coriander leaves. Serve.

16 – Doi Potol

Makes: 4 Servings

Cooking + Prep Time: 35 minutes

The list of ingredients:

- 1 tsp. of coriander powder
- 1 tsp. of turmeric powder
- 4 tbsp. of plain yogurt
- 1 tsp. of granulated sugar
- Clove, green cardamom, and cinnamon

- 1 x 1 pound gourd (potol)
- 1 tbsp. of ginger paste
- 1/2 tsp. of red chili powder
- 1/2 tsp. of powdered garam masala spice blend
- 2 tsp. of sea salt, +/- as desired
- 1 tsp. of cumin powder
- 1/4 tsp. of whole cumin
- 2 tbsp. of cashew paste
- 1 or 2 medium bay leaves

To garnish: 1 or 2 medium green chilies

- 3 tbsp. of vegetable oil

Method:

Step 1

Cut gourd ends. Scrape skin with veggie peeler. Make slits on vegetables. Smear a bit of salt turmeric to coat vegetables well. Set them aside.

Step 2

Add ginger paste, chili powder, coriander powder, cumin powder, turmeric powder, sugar and salt to small sized bowl. Add a bit of water. Mix well till you have a paste.

Step 3

Heat 2 tbsp. oil in wok. Reduce heat. Add potol. Fry
till light gold in color. Drain. Set aside.

Step 4

Add rest of oil. Add bay leaves and cumin seeds.
Wait till they are spluttering. Lower heat. Add
masala paste. Sauté for two to three minutes. Add
cashew paste. Add a bit of water so masala won't
stick to pan bottom.

Step 5

Cook masala for five to seven minutes, till oil and
masala separate. Whisk yogurt. Add to masala. Mix
well. Transfer fried gourd to gravy. Mix well.

Step 6

Add 1/2 cup water and allow gravy to boil. Reduce
heat and cover. Allow to cook for five minutes.
Check vegetable doneness with fork.

Step 7

Adjust seasoning as desired. Gravy should be
somewhat thick. Add garam masala powder. Turn off
heat. Cover. Allow to stand for about five minutes,
till flavors are blending well. Use chilies to garnish.
Transfer to serving dish. Serve while hot with
steamed rice.

17 – Bengali Spiced Crab Curry

Makes: 4 Servings

Cooking + Prep Time: 2 hours

The list of ingredients:

- 3 cups of sliced red onion

- 2 green cardamom pods

- 2 large, chopped tomatoes

- 2 tsp. of ground turmeric

- 5 whole black peppercorns

- 1 tbsp. of mustard seed

- 1 tsp. of white sugar

- 1 3/4 cups of peeled, halved, sliced potatoes

- 4 Thai green chilies

- 1 tbsp. of mustard oil

- 1 tsp. of cayenne pepper

- 1 1/2 tsp. of ginger paste

- 1 x 1" piece of cinnamon stick

- 1 1/2 tsp. of garlic paste

- 2 whole cloves

- Sea salt, as desired

- 1/2 tsp. of sea salt

- 1 tbsp. of hot water

- 2 cleaned, shell-cracked Dungeness crabs, fresh

For garnishing: 1/2 cup of fresh, chopped cilantro 1 fresh lemon wedge

Method:

Step 1

Rub crabs with 1/2 tsp. of sea salt 1 tsp. of turmeric. Allow to marinate for an hour.

Step 2

Combine hot water and mustard seed in bowl. Allow to sit for 10-12 minutes. Grind seeds into paste with mortar pestle.

Step 3

Heat oil in wok on med. heat. Add crabs. Stir fry till they have changed color, usually four to five minutes. Remove crabs. Set them aside.

Step 4

Add onions to wok. Stir while cooking on med. heat till onions become translucent. Raise heat up to high. Add potatoes. Cook and stir for a couple minutes.

Step 5

Add peppercorns, cardamom, cinnamon stick and cloves. Stir for 1/2 minute.

Step 6

Add and stir garlic and ginger pastes and tomatoes. Halve three chilies. Add to wok. Stir and cook for another one or two minutes on high heat. Lower heat to medium. Add remaining 1 tsp. of turmeric, mustard paste and cayenne pepper. Stir and combine.

Step 7

Add crabs to wok. Pour in water sufficient to cover

veggies. Bring water to boil. Stir in salt and sugar as desired.

Step 8

Cover wok. Reduce heat. Simmer till potatoes become tender and water has been reduced by 1/2. Remove lid. Stir. Simmer till gravy thickens.

Step 9

Squeeze lemon wedge over dish. Use sliced green chili and cilantro to garnish. Serve while hot, over rice.

18 – Bengali Sweet Potatoes

Makes: 4 Servings

Cooking + Prep Time: 40 minutes

The list of ingredients:

- 4 tbsp. of sunflower oil
- 2 to 4 sliced cloves of garlic
- 1 1/2 pound of peeled, chopped sweet potatoes
- 1 tbsp. of chopped coriander leaves

- 2 tsp. of panch phoron (Indian spice mixture)
- 1 large, sliced onion

Method:

Step 1

Boil the sweet potatoes till they become soft.

Step 2

Heat a skillet. Add oil. Stir fry panch phoron spice mix for a minute. Add garlic. Stir fry for a minute more.

Step 3

Add onion. Stir fry for about five minutes.

Step 4

Add coriander and sweet potatoes. Stir fry till ingredients have blended well and are all heated fully through. Season as desired. Serve promptly.

19 – Beef Samosas

Makes: 18 Servings

Cooking + Prep Time: 45 minutes

The list of ingredients:

- 4 crushed garlic cloves
- 2 tbsp. of chopped chili peppers
- 1 tbsp. of minced ginger root, fresh
- 1 ground tsp. each turmeric, coriander, and cumin

- 2 large, peeled potatoes

- 1 tsp. of chili powder

- 2 tbsp. of fresh chopped cilantro

- 1 1/2 tsp. of sea salt

- 1 crushed bay leaf

- 1/2 tsp. of ground pepper

- 2 tbsp. of vegetable oil

- 1/2 tsp. of ground cardamom

- 1/2 tsp. of cumin seeds

- 1/2 tsp. of ground cinnamon

- 2 large, chopped onions

- 1 cup of frozen, thawed peas

- 1 lb. of ground beef

To deep fry: 1 quart of oil

- 1 x 16-oz. pkg. of dough, phyllo

Method:

Step 1

Bring pan of salted water to boil. Add and stir peas and potatoes. Cook till potatoes are firm but tender. Drain. Mash potatoes and peas. Set aside.

Step 2

Heat oil in large pan on med-high. Brown the bay leaf and cumin seeds. Add ground beef and onions. Cook till beef has browned evenly and onions are soft.

Step 3

Add and mix in the ginger root and garlic. Season with cardamom, cinnamon, chili powder, turmeric, coriander, cumin, salt and pepper. Add and stir potato mixture. Remove it from the heat. Chill in fridge for an hour, till cool.

Step 4

Heat the oil in large pan on high heat.

Step 5

Mix green chili peppers and cilantro into beef and potato mixture. Place about one tbsp. of mixture on each of phyllo sheets. Fold the sheets into large triangles and press edges to seal.

Step 6

Fry phyllo till a golden brown in color in small sized batches. Drain on plate of paper towels. Serve while warm.

20 – Adipolia Parathas

Makes: 8 Servings

Cooking + Prep Time: 1 hour 55 minutes

The list of ingredients:

For dough

- 1/4 cup of vegetable oil
- 2/3 cup of filtered water
- 2 cups of whole wheat flour

For filling

- 1/2 tsp. of mustard seeds
- 2 large beaten eggs
- 1/2 tsp. of ground turmeric
- 1 1/2" piece of grated ginger
- Sea salt, as desired
- 2 peeled, chopped onions
- 6 oz. of peeled, deveined prawns, uncooked
- 1/2 cup of vegetable oil
- 10 fresh curry leaves
- 1 chopped green chili pepper

Method:

Step 1

Place flour in medium bowl. Add and stir water and 1/4 cup oil gradually to make pliable, soft dough. Turn onto cutting board. Knead for four to five minutes, till smooth. Transfer dough to oiled bowl. Cover bowl and set aside for an hour.

Step 2

Heat 1/2 cup oil in fry pan on med low. Sprinkle in mustard seeds. When seeds begin popping, add and stir curry leaves, onions, ginger and chili.

Step 3

Stir occasionally while cooking till onions become soft. Add 1 pinch salt and turmeric and cook for one more minute. Mix in prawns. Stir occasionally while cooking till meat isn't transparent anymore and prawns become pink on outside. Remove from heat. Set them aside.

Step 4

Divide dough in eight portions of same size. Place 1 pc. in your hands. Roll into ball. Dust with flour lightly and place on cutting board. Roll out into very thin 8 1/2-inch diameter circle. Repeat with rest of the dough.

Step 5

Heat heavy skillet on med. heat. Use cooking spray or use oil to brush skillet.

Step 6

Stir beaten eggs into filling mixture with prawn. Place one dough circle in skillet. Spread 3 tbsp. filling over dough. Cook till bread bottom is browned.

Step 7

Reduce heat. Turn paratha over carefully. Cook for

Step 7

Reduce heat. Turn paratha over carefully. Cook for five more minutes till prawn mixture sticks well to paratha. Flip again, then transfer to cutting board.

Step 8

Roll paratha in cylinder, enclosing filling. Repeat with rest of the dough and prawn filling. Slice parathas in halves. Serve.

21 – Fish Egg Pakora

Makes: 4 Servings

Cooking + Prep Time: 35 minutes

The list of ingredients:

- 1/3 tsp. of ground turmeric
- 1 chopped, large onion
- 8 3/4 oz. of fish eggs
- 2 pinches of sea salt

- 1/3 tsp. of red chili powder

- 1/3 tsp. of garam masala spice blend

- 1 tbsp. of garlic-chili paste

- 2 cups of refined oil

- 1/4 cup of fresh coriander leaves

For main dish

- 1/3 cup of rice flour

- 1 cup of besan flour

Method:

Step 1

Mix all ingredients except oil in large sized bowl.

Step 2

Heat the oil in deep pan. Take small sized portions of fish egg mixture from step 1. Gently place in hot oil one at a time.

Step 3

Fry on med. flame for one minute. Flip and fry other side, too. Serve as is or with rice.

22 – Bengali Steamed Fish

Makes: 2-3 Servings

Cooking + Prep Time: 35 minutes

The list of ingredients:

For base

- 1 tbsp. of poppy seeds
- 2 tablespoons mustard oil

- 1 tsp. sea salt, +/- as desired

- 1/2 tsp. of ground turmeric

- 1 tbsp. of mustard seeds black

- 2 green chilies

- 2 tbsp. of mustard oil

- 1 tbsp. of whole cashews or sliced almonds

- 1/2 cup of yogurt, light

For fish garnishing

- 2 tbsp. of chopped cilantro

- 1 jalapeno pepper

- 1 1/2 lbs. of 2"-cut salmon filet, wild caught if available

Optional for drizzling: 1 tbsp. of mustard oil

Method:

Step 1

Place nuts, mustard, and poppy seeds in spice grinder. Grind till you have a powder with smooth texture.

Step 2

Place powder in food processor. Add yogurt, 3 tbsp.

filtered water, mustard oil, salt, turmeric and jalapeno. Grind into paste.

Step 3

Place salmon in small, glass dish. Pour sauce on it.

Step 4

Add 2 cups filtered water to Instant Pot. Place trivet over water. Place glass dish on trivet.

Step 5

Cover IP. Set to steam at 12 minutes. Allow steam to naturally release. Remove dish from IP.

Step 6

Use cilantro to garnish. Drizzle using mustard oil. Serve hot.

23 – Spicy Tamarind

Makes: 2 Servings

Cooking + Prep Time: 50 minutes

The list of ingredients:

- 2 cups of filtered water
- 1 cup of all-purpose flour
- 1 tsp. of refined oil
- 2 medium onions

- 1 tbsp. of fresh ginger
- 1 tbsp. of garlic
- 2 tbsp. of mustard oil
- 1 tbsp. of sweet peas
- 5 pinches of sea salt
- 6 medium potatoes

Method:

Step 1

Knead flour with water, salt, and oil. Make soft dough and set it aside.

Step 2

Boil potatoes until tender. Add peas.

Step 3

Grind garlic, onion and ginger, making paste.

Step 4

Add oil to pan. Stir fry paste. Add peas, potatoes and salt.

Step 5

Add 1 cup water. Boil till you have dry Aloor Dum (potato-based dish)

Step 6

Make small balls with dough. Roll into Luchi. Deep fry.

Step 7

Use green chili and lemon wedges to garnish. Serve.

74

24 – Prawn Curry

Makes: 2 Servings

Cooking + Prep Time: 45 minutes

The list of ingredients:

To prepare prawns

- 1 tsp. of turmeric powder
- 12 de-veined, de-shelled king prawns

* 1 tsp. of sea salt

* 1 tsp. of paprika powder

For masala/gravy

* 3 tbsp. of vegetable oil

Optional: 2 tbsp. of ghee

* 4 black peppercorns

* 2 inches of grated ginger

* 1 medium bay leaf

* 1/4 tsp. of granulated sugar

* 2 grated garlic cloves

* 1 tsp. of garam masala spice blend

* filtered Water

* 2 halved green bird eye chilies

* 1/3 quart of coconut milk

* 1 small, diced onion

* 1-inch stick of cinnamon

* 1/2 tsp. of hot paprika

* 3 cloves

* 1 tsp. of sea salt

Method:

Step 1

Place the prawns in medium bowl. Sprinkle with paprika, salt and turmeric. Combine thoroughly.

Step 2

Heat 3 tbsp. of oil in non-stick pan. Once oil is heated, add prawns. Cook over med. heat for two minutes. Prawns need to be white and firm. Remove them from pan.

Step 3

Heat ghee and mustard oil in pan. Once heated, add cumin, bay leaf, peppercorns, cloves and cinnamon stick.

Step 4

When spices start spluttering, add onions. Add 1/4 tsp. of sea salt. Cook for a few minutes, till onions become translucent. Add garlic and ginger. Cook for three to four more minutes, till golden brown in color.

Step 5

Add 2 tbsp. of filtered water, sugar, garam masala, turmeric, paprika and sea salt. Mix together, creating paste. Add to pan. Add green chilies. Combine well.

Step 6

Add 1 cup water and coconut milk. Bring to a boil. Reduce heat immediately. Simmer for three to four minutes. Check seasoning and adjust as desired.

Step 7

Add prawns. Let them simmer for three to four minutes. Turn heat off. Serve.

25 – Coriander Leaf Paste with Rice

Makes: 2 Servings

Cooking + Prep Time: 30 minutes

The list of ingredients:

- 3 or 4 green chilies
- 1/2 tsp. of garlic paste
- 1 fat bunch of washed, chopped coriander leaves
- 1/2 tsp. of dry mango powder

- Sea salt, as desired

- 2 tbsp. of mustard oil

- Rice

Method:

Step 1

Add chilies and coriander to mixer. Mix till you have a coarse paste.

Step 2

Heat mustard oil in fry pan. Add mango powder, coriander paste, garlic paste and a bit of salt.

Step 3

Stir continuously for four to five minutes over med-high flame. Allow extra liquid in coriander paste to completely evaporate. When paste becomes a darker color, it is done. Remove it from heat. Serve on hot rice.

Want to taste some original treats? Try one of these Bengali desserts...

26 – Bhaja Pithe

Makes: 5 Servings

Cooking + Prep Time: 2 hours

The list of ingredients:

For dough

- 1 cup of boiled, split yellow moong dal
- rice flour, as needed

- 1 pinch of sea salt

- 1 tsp. of whole wheat flour

- 1 1/2 tsp. of sesame seeds

- 1/2 tsp. of cumin powder

- 2 boiled sweet potatoes

For deep frying

- cooking oil

For the filling

- 1 1/2 cups of brown sugar

- 2 cardamom pods

- 1 cup of fresh coconut

For serving

- Jaggery sugar

Method:

Step 1

Dry roast the jaggery and coconut. Stir till done and fragrant. Set aside.

Step 2

Mash boiled sweet potatoes and boiled moon dal in bowl.

Step 3

Add sesame seeds, cumin powder, salt and jaggery. Combine well.

Step 4

Add rice and wheat flours to create a soft dough.

Step 5

Use soft dough to create small balls. Flatten them in palm with finger and thumb, making bowl shapes.

Step 6

Stuff in coconut filling. Close edges.

Step 7

Deep fry shapes in oil over med. flame till golden brown. Deep fry them in batches.

Step 8

Allow to cool. Drizzle over with liquid jaggery. Serve.

27 – Mishti Doi

Makes: 4-6 Servings

Cooking + Prep Time: 45 minutes

The list of ingredients:

- 3 to 4 tbsp. of light yogurt
- 8 3/4 oz. of white sugar
- 1 quart of full cream whole milk

Method:

Step 1

> Boil milk in heavy pan over med. flame till reduced to 1/2 original volume. Stir frequently so milk won't scorch. Cool milk when done.

Step 2

> Place sugar in separate pan. Heat on low flame and melt. Allow sugar to brown. Remove from heat after done. Add reduced milk. Combine well.

Step 3

> When sugar and milk have mixed well, add yogurt. Mix gently.

Step 4

> Pour in container. Keep in dark, warm spot so it will set. After mixture is firm and set, chill for several hours. Serve.

28 – Poha Pudding

Makes: 6 Servings

Cooking + Prep Time: 50 minutes

The list of ingredients:

- 1 tbsp. of raisins
- 1/2 cup of flattened rice (poha)
- 2 1/2 quarts of whole milk
- 8-10 chopped cashews or almonds

- 1 cup of brown sugar

- 1 pinch sea salt

- 2 cardamom pods

- 2 tbsp. of rice flour

- 1 pinch of Saffron strands + extra for garnishing

Method:

Step 1

Wash the poha and strain it.

Step 2

Soak washed, drained poha in 1 cup of milk.

Step 3

Mix 1/2 cup milk with flour. Set aside.

Step 4

Soak saffron in a bit of milk and set it aside.

Step 5

Boil remainder of cardamom pods and milk together in pan. Bring to a boil. Stir it occasionally.

Step 6

Add flour mix into boiling milk, constantly stirring.

Step 7

Boil for 12-25 minutes till milk has condensed and rice flour has cooked.

Step 8

Add poha and milk-soaked saffron.

Step 9

Cook for 12-15 more minutes. Add brown sugar.

Step 10

Stir mixture. Cook till brown sugar has dissolved.
Add nuts and pinch of sea salt. Cook for one minute.
Remove from heat.

Step 11

Pour in serving bowl and use nuts, raisins and strands
of saffron to garnish. Serve.

29 – Pan Laddu

Makes: 2-3 Servings

Cooking + Prep Time: 15 minutes

The list of ingredients:

- 1 tbsp. of gulkand (rose petals sugar)
- 6 condensed milks
- 1 1/2 cup of coconut powder + 1/4 cup to coat
- 1 tbsp. food coloring, green

- 14 oz. of ghee
- Betel

Method:

Step 1

Add chopped betel to mixing jar. Add milk. Make a paste.

Step 2

Place pan over low heat. Add coconut powder and ghee. Roast for a couple minutes while stirring. Add betel paste and mix well. Add food coloring. Mix well.

Step 3

Continue to stir till the mixture is lumpy and thick. Remove from heat when mixture starts separating from pan. Place on separate plate. Allow it to cool down.

Step 4

Remove dough by small handfuls and make ball shapes. Dip in coconut powder for coating. Make remainder of dough the same. Serve.

Makes: 4-6 Servings

Cooking + Prep Time: 2 hours 10 minutes

The list of ingredients:

- 1 3/4 oz. of raisins
- 1 tsp. of cardamom powder
- 1 3/4 oz. of blanched, slivered nuts
- 1 cup white sugar

- Several saffron strands
- 2 quarts of full-cream milk
- 1 cup Basmati rice
- 1 can of sweetened and condensed milk

Method:

Step 1

Wash rice. Soak for 30 minutes in water.

Step 2

Put sugar, condensed milk and milk in deep pan. Boil. Add rice, then simmer. Cook till milk has thickened and reduced to 1/2 its volume.

Step 3

Add cardamom and nuts. Cook for five minutes more.

Step 4

Remove from heat. Add saffron. Combine. Allow mixture to cool and then chill. Serve while cold.

www.ingramcontent.com/pod-product-compliance
Lightning Source LLC
Chambersburg PA
CBHW071546150726
48000CB00002B/965